TREVA J

WHEN A

WOMAN
PRAYS

SHE MAKES HELL MAD

21-Day Devotional Journal

ELOHAI
INTERNATIONAL
PUBLISHING & MEDIA

Published by ELOHAI International Publishing & Media:
P.O. Box 1883
Cypress, TX 77433
elohaipublishing.com

For inquiries or to request bulk copies, e-mail hello@elohaiintl.com.

Scriptures marked AMP are taken from the AMPLIFIED BIBLE (AMP): Scripture taken from the AMPLIFIED® BIBLE, Copyright © 1954, 1958, 1962, 1964, 1965, 1987 by the Lockman Foundation Used by Permission. (www.Lockman.org)

Scriptures marked ESV are taken from the THE HOLY BIBLE, ENGLISH STANDARD VERSION (ESV): Scriptures taken from THE HOLY BIBLE, ENGLISH STANDARD VERSION® Copyright © 2001 by Crossway, a publishing ministry of Good News Publishers. Used by permission.

Scriptures marked KJV are taken from the KING JAMES VERSION (KJV): KING JAMES VERSION, public domain.

Scriptures marked NIV are taken from the NEW INTERNATIONAL VERSION (NIV): Scripture taken from THE HOLY BIBLE, NEW INTERNATIONAL VERSION®. Copyright © 1973, 1978, 1984, 2011 by Biblica, Inc.™. Used by permission of Zondervan.

Scriptures marked NKJV are taken from the NEW KING JAMES VERSION (NKJV): Scripture taken from the NEW KING JAMES VERSION®. Copyright © 1982 by Thomas Nelson, Inc. Used by permission. All rights reserved.

Scriptures marked NLT are taken from the HOLY BIBLE, NEW LIVING TRANSLATION (NLT): Scriptures taken from the HOLY BIBLE, NEW LIVING TRANSLATION, Copyright © 1996, 2004, 2007 by Tyndale House Foundation. Used by permission of Tyndale House Publishers, Inc., Carol Stream, Illinois 60188. All rights reserved. Used by permission.

ISBN: 978-1-953535-65-8

Printed in the United States of America

DEDICATION

I dedicate this book to my uncle, the Late E.P. Riley. He always said, "Keep going, don't stop, and never go back to the familiar. In the familiar, it's nothing there, baby." His words have been my push and motivation to keep collecting everything that's for me.

I pray his words will be as big of a blessing to you as they are to me. May you stay encouraged and motivated because God is not finished!

"Everything Is Everything."

TABLE OF CONTENTS

ACKNOWLEDGEMENTS

My Husband

Thank you, honey, for being my support, help, strength, encouragement, and motivation. With every idea I presented, you never told me I couldn't do it but encouraged me to go after it when I did not believe it was possible. Our journey has not been easy, but we have learned to trust God with our marriage, life, and family during the good and bad. I thank you most of all for allowing me to be me and tolerating me as your wife and lifelong partner.

I am beyond proud to call you my husband. I love you beyond this life.

My Three

Where do I begin? I would like to thank the three of you for pushing me even when I did not know where I was going. For understanding that when I took off running to my notebook, I had an idea or message that needed to be written down immediately. Thank you for understanding the importance of my prayer time and allowing me to lay in the presence of God for as long as I needed to. I love you all so much!

My Mother

Ma, I love you to the moon and back; you are my rock. Thank you for showing me the strength of a wife and mother. Even in your weakest moments, you somehow found strength. Little did I know God was pouring his strength upon you. You have listened to me vent, pulled on my anointing, and taught and helped me to grow in ways I could have never fathomed. I am so grateful to call you Mom. I love you, and thank you for always being there and never judging me!

Last but not least, I would like to thank all those who have spoken into my life, supported, encouraged, and motivated me. Special thanks to Jas, who held me accountable all the way down to the deadline. To Kendra for being obedient and birthing Committed to Consistency. To Sharika and LaSondra for not letting me forget about the assignment. To all of you, I'm grateful and honored to call you my family!

INTRODUCTION

WHEN A WOMAN PRAYS, she prays and covers her home in its entirety. As women, we should set the atmosphere and tone daily, leaving no room for the enemy but open space for the Holy Spirit. I want to personally encourage each woman to constantly seek after God. Find scriptures that you are able to stand on and declare over your home, marriage, children, etc. Always remember if married, we are called to be helpmeets unto our spouses and knowing that what we do unto them, we do to God. By the end of this devotion, my prayer is that we will have grown a little and have learned a lot more. May you challenge yourself to search YOU with all honesty. Some of the questions can be very challenging, but the key is understanding the power of prayer and being able to overcome hard times in your life while praying. I had to check myself as well regarding some of the questions asked because we can be so quick to question someone else. God has taught me to check me first before sharing with other people. I'm not a minister and have no theology degree; however, what I do have is a heart for people. To be given the honor to share my life, experiences, and prayers with others makes me beyond grateful.

May God cover and protect you. In Jesus' name, amen.

Please allow this devotion to minister to you over the next twenty-one days of your life.

HEALING PRAYER

When a wife prays, she covers some of the deepest things. Today, I would like to pray for all of our healing. We know that we can't grow properly in a wounded place. We have all heard that hurt people hurt people, so before we start these twenty-one days, I would like to say a special prayer over you.

Father, I thank you today for this opportunity to be here to share life and a new day. Father, I thank you for your son, Jesus. Lord, I come touching and agreeing for the wounded woman, wife, sister, daughter, and/or friend. I pray that she will search herself and acknowledge the past and/or present hurt. Lord, I pray because she was able to be truthful and transparent that you will start her on her healing journey. Father, I know it's not an overnight process, but it is a step to being a better person. So today, we, I _____ (make it personal) let go of bitterness, anger, trust issues, etc.

Lord, I pray you will heal the little girl who has been hurt on the inside. The little girl who longed after her father, who has caused her to date so many men. Lord, I pray for the little girl who fights with insecurities. Lord, heal her first so you can work on the awesome, beautiful, courageous, and fearfully and wonderfully made woman you created her to be. Father, I pray that the healing will start now from the inside out, and, Father, that you shall cover her home and marriage as she seeks you and prays more during these next few weeks. I declare on this day, _____, that you are walking into your freedom and healing in the mighty name of Jesus. Amen.

Day 1

STRENGTH

We are all faced with challenges that may weaken us. Some moments are longer than others, but what do we do when we have no more push or strength to move beyond that moment?

As a mom and wife, I have to pray and find out the area where I fall weak. After a self-search, I go into prayer because my strength comes from God. Only in his presence will I receive the strength I need to move beyond that moment. With no strength, I feel robbed of my freedom to overcome obstacles. It's like running in a track meet. If you are not conditioned mentally and physically, you can fall weak during the race. If you condition yourself mentally and physically (through practices and meditating on the Word of God), then you will feel the wind and strength needed to pursue the race. The scripture tells us when we are weak, God is strong (being weak physically means God can show up spiritually). The flesh and the spirit are always at war, but if we lay down our flesh during the weak moments, the spirit of God that dwells on the inside will show us strength like no other.

2 Corinthians 12: 9-10 (NKJV)

And He said to me, "My grace is sufficient for you, for My strength is made perfect in weakness." Therefore most gladly I will rather boast in my infirmities, that the power of Christ may rest upon me.

We all have been in that place where we have no strength to go on. We literally have been through hell and hot water, but we are told if we hold on a little longer, we will reach the finish line. How many times can you say you threw in the towel just before God blessed you? Can you remember a time when God gave you strength and you definitely knew it was him? If so, how did it make you feel?

_____

_____

_____

_____

_____

_____

_____

_____

_____

_____

_____

_____

_____

_____

Day 2
PEACE CONSUME ME

We all have those days when we think we cannot catch a break. You may feel like the world has come down or even wonder when this will end. Can I let you know you are not alone? Those days find me as well. There are times I'm sleepless and just on the edge, if I can be honest. I know my peace has been taken in those moments, and I honestly do not like living in a sad, peace-deprived place. I will find any and everything to fill the void. At times, I looked for a quick fix by using marijuana, which only numbs the feeling for a moment. After encountering God on a more personal level, I surrendered and said, "God, I cannot keep feeling like this. I need peace in my life and my mind." I realized then that the peace I was missing came from him.

John 16:33 (KJV)
These things I have spoken unto you, that in me ye might have peace. In the world you will have tribulation, but be of good cheer: I have overcome the world.

Have you ever been in a place where you felt like you had been robbed of your peace? If so, how did you handle it?

_____

_____

_____

_____

_____

_____

_____

_____

_____

_____

_____

_____

_____

_____

_____

_____

Day 3
I NEED YOUR JOY

We have all heard "this joy that I have, the world did not give it to me, and the world cannot take it away," or can it?

Well, it depends on how you look at it. Nothing can be taken from a person unless that person invites the borrower into their world. God is a restoring God, and He gives back anything that is lost, stolen, and/or borrowed. I remember when I used to get up at 4 a.m. I would pick up my friend to drop her off at work and then pick up my sister-in-law from work and drive her home.

One morning she asked, "Girl, why are you so happy in the morning?"

I replied, "Girl, I do not know. I woke up like this."

A few days later, I understood it was joy, and I felt like I was drowning in it. I just wanted to touch everyone I met so they could feel the joy I had been experiencing.

Romans 15:13 (NIV)

May the God of hope fill you with all joy and peace as you trust in him, so that you (I, we) may overflow with hope by the power of the Holy Spirit.

How do you define joy? Have you been so unhappy but could never find a solution for the emotions you were experiencing? What if I told you that what you needed was at your fingertips? What if I told you that joy trumps sadness every time? Would you believe me if I told you that joy was not in the world but in God? How can you get to that place? Are joy and happiness the same?

_____

_____

_____

_____

_____

_____

_____

_____

_____

_____

_____

_____

_____

_____

_____

_____

Day 4
CHILDREN

If you are a mother, then maybe you will agree with me to some extent. We are living in a time when we have to monitor our children's every move due to all the things taking place around us. As the mother of a melanin boy, I fear every move he makes and every time he opens his mouth. As the mother of two girls, I fear the thought of them being kidnapped. That is how the enemy traps us as well. God never designed us to live in fear of those things listed above, but the truth is we do. Being a mother is one of the toughest jobs to hold because we take the definition of "superhero" to another level. We are protectors, and we love our babies to the core. If anything comes against our children, we also know how to fight for them. I educate my children on not just the Word of God but the things of the world as well.

Proverbs 22:6 (ESV)

Train up a child in the way he should go: even when he is old, he will not depart from it.

Develop a personal prayer that you can declare over your children

What are some fears you have pertaining to your children?

Do you think as parents we should educate them on things such as senseless killings, sex trafficking, family molestation, etc.? If yes, why?

_____

_____

_____

_____

_____

_____

_____

_____

_____

_____

_____

_____

_____

_____

_____

_____

Day 5
RENEW AND RESTORE

Often, we easily conform to people around us, but God wants us to change the atmosphere and those around us. He wants us to be the light in the dark places we enter. John 1: 5 tells us that darkness cannot comprehend the light.

The word comprehend comes from the Greek word *Katalambano*, which means acquire, grasp, or lay hold of. Light represents the knowledge, which comes from the Word of God (just a little *Trevaology*, my own opinion). Jesus was the Word, and those he often encountered did not believe he was the Word and the light. We have to be sober-minded (sensible) so we can function in a way that will help the household flow as normal. If the husband and wife are both consumed in the mind, then who will be able to cover the home? It's just like being on watch. While my husband was on deployment, I told him not to be focused on things in the states because there was a war going on in his presence. He needed to be focused physically, mentally, and spiritually. Worrying about things emotionally could have caused casualties on his behalf. So being renewed and restored in the mind daily is important because when we wake each morning, we never know what the day may bring.

Romans 12:2 (KJV)

And be not conformed to this world: but be ye transformed by the renewing of your mind, that ye may prove what *is* that good, and acceptable, and perfect, will of God.

When was your last update?

Many times, we do a factory reset but do not ask for an upgrade or update. With a phone or computer, we may have to reset due to a virus or a system slow down. The device prompts us to update, and if we never update, we will not experience the device (God) to its full capacity.

Are you ready for a reset? Why?

_____

_____

_____

_____

_____

_____

_____

_____

_____

_____

_____

_____

_____

_____

Day 6

FAITH

We have all been asked if we will trust God even when we cannot trace God. The spiritual response is yes, but physically, my answer used to be no since we are being honest.

Back in 2013, I facilitated a prayer line that started off as prayer but ended up as a midweek service. On the call, I taught about faith faithfully, and I asked my husband how could I be giving a word for people, when God's Word was not active in my own home. At that moment, I realized that the words *have faith* weren't just for people who called the line but for me and my home first. It wasn't until I went through some of the same things I was teaching that I began to walk in faith. Through many nights of being taught through my dreams, I eventually was put to the test.

In 2013, we had a new baby. When she was about six months, I somehow lost her WIC folder. My husband had just joined the military and I had no job, so we were really living paycheck to paycheck with three children. I looked everywhere and could not find her vouchers. When I called the clinic, they told me there was nothing they could do. As a mother, I was hurt and mad. I told my neighbors I lost the baby's WIC folder but didn't tell them our financial status because I did not think it was important.

I prayed and then laid down. My sister called, and we talked for a little while. While on the phone with her, I received a call from my neighbors to come outside. When I went outside, they were standing with cans of milk for the baby. At that moment, I could have passed out because God showed himself strong when I was weak. I started praising on the phone with my sister because I had started to trust God when I couldn't trace him.

2 Corinthians 5:7 (KJV)

For we walk by faith, not by sight.

Father, I pray for the mother, wife, fiancé, or sister reading this. Lord, I pray that you will increase their faith in you, God. Lord, your Word says in Matthew 17:20 that if we have faith the size of a mustard seed, we can speak to mountains and say come down, and they shall come down due to our faith. Lord, I ask for protection over them right now in the name of Jesus as they learn to trust you, Father, that they won't lack anything. Father, I pray as they decrease their own fleshly desires, Lord, you increase your will in their lives, that their faith level will be more than a mustard seed because they love and trust you the most. Father, as they read or pray, cover them from the top of their heads to the soles of their feet. In your son Jesus' name, I pray that my sister will walk in faith. In Jesus' gracious name I pray, amen.

So are you willing to trust God when you cannot trace him? If you struggle with your faith, I believe that if you pray and ask God to strengthen you in that area, then he will. Take this time to create your own faith declaration of prayer for your faith journey.

_____

_____

_____

_____

_____

_____

_____

_____

_____

_____

_____

_____

_____

_____

_____

Day 7

GODLY WISDOM

I am always looking for more wisdom. As the person people always come to for advice or prayer, I never want to just say anything, especially when it's a person's life. Godly wisdom is needed, especially being married, waiting to get married, or becoming a mom. We just need wisdom in everything we do. You never want to go into something with no education. Being married has its ups and downs, but knowing that it gets better is worth it all. If no one had ever told me there would be arguments in marriage, I think I would be broken into pieces. The Bible tells us in Genesis that God made Adam a helpmeet, and Adam called her woman. According to Genesis 2:23, Adam said, "Now this is bone of my bone and flesh of my flesh because she was taken from man." Without the knowledge of Genesis, we would not have the understanding of husband and wife. As a wife, I'm constantly growing because I personally believe wisdom is learned through trial. So we will never have all the wisdom. That's why we seek God for instructions, history, and knowledge on things we do not know.

Proverbs 2:6-7 (NLT)

For the LORD grants wisdom! From his mouth come knowledge and understanding. He grants a treasure of common sense to the honest. He is a shield to those who walk with integrity.

What are you seeking God's wisdom, knowledge, and understanding about? What has been God's response?

I do know to properly understand a thing, person, or situation, we must have knowledge and wisdom. Wisdom means to have research or experience, so we can have the knowledge to properly understand. We cannot have one without the other; they work together.

_____

_____

_____

_____

_____

_____

_____

_____

_____

_____

_____

_____

_____

_____

Day 8

WHERE THERE IS GOD, THERE IS UNITY

God is the center of all things; nothing functions properly without God, and if it is functioning, it will soon fall. Matthew 7:24-27 talks about the importance of building on a solid foundation. A foundation is not just a church but your home and marriage as well. I have been in a place where I thought God was the center. I had become comfortable with what was my normal atmosphere, but I didn't realize when God was no longer the center. God had to call me to the forefront because I was not focused. At that point, I realized the brokenness of the foundation in, not just my home, but my marriage as well.

The unity had been broken, and I prayed many nights for it to be restored. In God-ordained relationships, there must be some type of unity. I'm not saying that there will not be any problems, because there will be. God's building (house, marriage, ministry, job, etc.) will always stand. I had to find where the cracks were. I had to seek God on how to rebuild because I didn't know where to start or how. God gave me strength like never before. I was reminded that what is broken can be fixed. With careful instructions, God did just that. I had to allow God to remove all the corrosion and dried-out beams. I had to allow God to replace and seal up all the footings to make a more solid foundation, and the process did not start with my spouse but with me first. During that season, I learned God had to fix my spouse and me separately and then collectively for us to operate in unity.

Being in a place of solidarity with your spouse and household brings a new level of peace and respect. So I thank God for the brokenness of the foundation because without leaks, I wouldn't be able to pray for reconstruction mentally, physically, emotionally, and spiritually.

Philippians 2:2 (NIV)

Then make my joy complete by being like-minded, having the same love, being one in spirit and of one mind.

What is unity: the state of being united— joined as a whole

Have you been in a place that caused your foundation to shift or to become rocky? If so, how did you rebuild?

_____

_____

_____

_____

_____

_____

_____

_____

_____

_____

_____

_____

_____

_____

_____

Day 9
WIFE

Since about the age of fifteen, my best friend and I have planned our weddings, like other young girls our age. We would take pictures out of magazines and write in detail how we wanted our weddings to be, and I'm sure we picked our husbands as well. One of the things we didn't read up on was the role of a wife and the things a wife may go through. I grew up in a home where I was not taught to be a wife but was taught to be strong during adverse times. Becoming a wife is easy, but understanding what a wife is can be hard if you do not have any clear advice. There are many things a wife should and shouldn't be. Since I grew up in an abusive home, I have learned a lot of things from trial and error. Those times made me a better wife and deepened my relationship with God.

One of my favorite scriptures is Proverbs 14: 1, which reads, "Every wise woman buildeth her house: but the foolish plucketh it down with her hands." (OUCH)

Now, this day is a lot longer than the others on purpose. I know there were a lot of things I had to learn through trial and error, so I wanted to go a little deeper.

Proverbs 31:10-12

And the LORD God said, *It is* not good that the man should be alone; I will make him an help meet for him.

The Woman Who Fears the Lord
10
[a] An excellent wife who can find?
She is far more precious than jewels.

11

The heart of her husband trusts in her,
and he will have no lack of gain.

12

She does him good, and not harm,
all the days of her life.

Are you in a place to **be** someone's help**meet**? If you answered yes, have you learned to be alone? Have you learned to love yourself? Have you forgiven past relationships that hurt?

1. Do you understand what a wife is in its entirety? If you answered yes, what is a wife?

2. Are you or were you like me and had to learn through error? If you answered yes, what did you learn?

3. Are you in a place now where you feel like a foolish wife and need to know how to restore yourself? If you answered yes, think about the real you and every flaw you have. Now think about the mistakes you make as a wife or fiancé. At some point, if you are being honest, you should be asking God to forgive you for all that you have done as a wife or fiancé that hasn't pleased him. Remember what we do to our spouse, we do to God.

_____

_____

_____

_____

_____

Day 10

DEAR HUSBAND,

It is important for wives to cover their husbands daily. I once heard Prophetess Valerie Moore minister that a man's best comes from him while he is asleep.

God caused Adam to fall into a deep sleep to create him a helpmeet. Adam spoke in Genesis 2:23-24, saying, "This is now bone of my bones and flesh of my flesh: she shall be called woman, because she was taken out of man."

For many years, I thought that the ribs protect the lungs, which is a vital organ, but in a late-night live, Prophetess Moore explained that the ribs protect first the heart and secondly the lungs. She then explained how if the lungs were ever punctured, it would cause the husband to slowly suffocate.

That blew my mind because I never thought about what would ever happen if my husband's lungs and heart were to ever be punctured or exposed spiritually. Wives must be aware of the anatomy of not just our physical body and or nature, but spiritual as well. We must fully understand our full potential as wives and covering for our husbands.

Genesis 2:18 (KJV)

And the LORD God said, *It is* not good that the man should be alone; I will make him an help meet for him.

Have you ever been in a place where your husband's heart was exposed spiritually? I learned that there are two ways a husband can break his wife. Not just break her heart, but first external, which will expose the husband's heart, then internal, which will puncture his lungs. As a wife, have you ever been broken to the point where your husband suffocated spiritually? If so, did you cover him in prayer as God performed his miracle? Are you willing to learn from your husband?

_____

_____

_____

_____

_____

_____

_____

_____

_____

_____

_____

_____

_____

_____

_____

Day 11

BALANCE: THE WEIGHT OF IT ALL

I need to do this, I have to go here, I need to go there. They ask me to participate in this while doing all those things for everybody else. The place you call home is being neglected, and we never want to get to the point where home is not attended to. When I realized I had no balance, it was too late. My son had gone through three teachers within the first two months of school, and my marriage was on life support. Yes, I said my marriage was on life support, and I did not even know that it was wounded, or shall I say I didn't pay attention to the wounds that not just my marriage received, but my home as well. It took me a full two years to understand balance, and if it meant cutting off relationships with people, I did that. Some people didn't understand, but I wasn't in a place to share the separation due to balancing my spiritual walk as well. When we weigh priorities, some carry more weight than others, and the priorities that weigh the most (marriage, relationships, children) are what we need to evaluate and value most.

Trevaology: I believe there is a time for everything, and some seasons are just for one thing, whether it's to focus on your marriage, children, growth, business, etc. We must find balance for those things that matter most; if not, we will lose them.

Ecclesiastes 3:1 (KJV)

To every *thing there is* a season, and a time to every purpose under the heaven:

Are you willing to release the weight that is causing you back pains? Just like the lady who suffered from an infirmity for twelve long years, who was aching and bowed over. She did what was needed to be healed and released the weight that had her stagnant for years. Why is it weighing you down? Is it because you think you need it, or is it memories you do not want to let go?

Why can't I find a place for it all in my life?

_____

_____

_____

_____

_____

_____

_____

_____

_____

_____

_____

_____

_____

_____

Day 12
FINANCES

I know you have heard, "I have to rob Peter to pay Paul." We all go through our dry spells when we may not know how we are going to pay all the bills for the month. We then start strategizing on what's important and thinking about what we can go without. Believe it or not, finances can be a huge burden in marriage.

I remember being in New York praying and asking God to show me how to be good with our finances. Since my husband was the only person working, we needed to balance out at the end of the month. God began to show me increase, and he told me, "You have to be faithful and manageable over the little." So I was moved to get all our bills pushed to the middle of the month, ranging from the fifteenth to the twenty-third. I then opened a sub-account titled bills, so when my husband got paid, I moved all the bill money to the sub-account. Our bills were totaled and split down the middle, which we took from the main account on the first and the fifteenth. Since we have direct deposit, that gave us a day or two grace period. Those funds were deposited into the bills account, so when bills were due, all funds were accounted for. That system worked and still works for our household. I remember being in the car at the gas station, and my husband asked whether I paid all the bills.

"Yes," I said, "Is something wrong?"

"We have more money in the bank," he said.

Being young in our second year of marriage, we were still figuring it out.

I pulled out my little notebook to check everything and said, "Yes, everything checks out."

It then hit me. God had taught me finances; I was so excited

at that moment because we were able to breathe. Months passed
and our bank account got hacked. Oh my goodness! Again, I was
reminded God had taught me finances. I immediately said, "Now,
God, I was not talking about this way." Just a few months before, we
were led to open up another account. At the moment, the "teach me
finances" lesson evolved to a "trust God lesson. It was kind of bad,
but by trusting God and much prayer, we overcame that obstacle.
During those financial crisis, I have always been reminded of many
scriptures, but there's one that works for me:

Philippians 4:19 (KJV)

But my God shall supply all your (MY) need according to his riches
in glory by Christ Jesus.

This lets me know that I will always be supplied with everything I need.

Father in heaven, I pray that you increase every reader's finances.
God, we decree and declare that they will be debt-free. Father, I pray
for an increase in credit scores that the favor of you, God, will reign
so heavy upon their lives that they will be able to drive off the lot
with brand-new vehicles of their choice, Lord. With a low payment,
low interest rate, better yet, paid in full in the name of Jesus. Lord,
I pray for the homeowners, that they will get the houses of their
dreams, Lord, that they will not have to settle, Father. I pray that they
will be lenders and not borrowers. Lord, that you are educating and
equipping them to create generational wealth for their children's children. God, we pray for their businesses and increase in every area of
their lives. Lord, everyone connected to them shall be blessed. Father,
Proverbs 10:22 declares: "The Lord's blessing makes a person rich,
and your Father adds no sorrow." So in the mighty name of Jesus, we
decree and declare it. In your son's name I pray, amen.

Do you struggle with balancing finances? If so, have you found a solution? I suggest adopting the solution that helped my household balance. Are you and your husband comfortable with discussing finances? I suggest taking time to collectively come together and discuss finances monthly.

Create a prayer or find a scripture that you can recite as motivation that reminds you God is your provider.

_____

_____

_____

_____

_____

_____

_____

_____

_____

_____

_____

_____

_____

Day 13
INTIMACY

The best is yet to come. The word intimacy comes from the Latin word *intimus*, which means inmost, innermost, deepest. Intimacy is being able to open up and connect with someone physically, mentally, emotionally, and/or spiritually. Many times, people look at being intimate as being sexual, but wives have to learn to be with their spouses mentally, emotionally, as well as spiritually. If you are able to meet your spouse in all those areas, it will be just as satisfying physically. In Hebrew, the word intimacy means closeness.

Once my husband and I were talking, and I told him if he could be intimate with God the way he tried to be intimate with me, he would understand. God flipped that thing on me and told me, "If you can be as intimate with your husband as you are with me, maybe you will understand." Oh my goodness! My husband will tell you I just said, "Oh, never mind," and it was like he knew what God had spoken because he replied, "Yeah, alright then." I could have passed out, but it would not be God if he did not correct us when we are wrong. That is the best part about having an intimate relationship with God even when you are wrong. He still loves you just as a husband or wife is supposed to love his or her spouse. We have to learn our spouse's love language so we can meet them on a more intimate level.

1 Corinthians 7:3-5 (KJV)

Let the husband render unto the wife due benevolence: and likewise also the wife unto the husband. The wife hath not power of her own body, but the husband: and likewise also the husband hath not power of his own body, but the wife. Defraud ye not one the other, except *it be* with consent for a time, that ye may give yourselves to fasting and prayer; and come together again, that Satan tempt you not for your incontinency.

Do you know your spouse's love language? Have you taken the time to learn your spouse on a more intimate (not sexual) level? When was the last time you and your spouse had a romantic night? A night where you focused on each other, a moment where you both just connected and remembered your reason for marriage—The Why?

_____

_____

_____

_____

_____

_____

_____

_____

_____

_____

_____

_____

_____

Day 14

LOVE

The word love gets thrown around a lot, with no action behind it. I believe people use the word love because at a young age, we are taught to say, "I love you." Think about it—as mothers, we say to our babies, "Mommy loves you." We say it so much that it becomes a learned word, just like mommy and daddy. I remember going through marriage counseling, and our pastor asked my husband and me, "What is love?" We both gave our definition, and he replied, "Those are great, but love is to die for." I thought to myself, *Well, wait a minute, is this somebody I'm willing to die for? Is this really the husband God has for me?*

He then began to tell us love was demonstrated when Jesus died on the cross. God loved us so much that he gave his only son so we may live (John 3:16). It wasn't until I grew spiritually that I was able to understand love in its entirety. As a mother, I will die for my children if I can sacrifice my life so they can live. Since I'm married to an awesome husband who works to risk his life for all, I would sacrifice my life for him to live if I had to. I know he would make sure our children are loved, educated, and taken care of properly. Most of all, love is dying to self, daily, so we can be in a place to love others and receive love properly. So when we say we love someone, it should not be just for show, but it should be followed by action. Teaching your children what love is, what it looks like—verses just saying it is different. Love does not hurt or cause pain.

1 Corinthians 13:4-8 (NLT)

Love is patient and kind. Love is not jealous or boastful or proud or rude. It does not demand its own way. It is not irritable, and it keeps no record of being wronged. It does not rejoice about injustice but rejoices whenever the truth wins out. Love never gives up, never loses faith, is always hopeful, and endures through every circumstance.

Prophecy and speaking in unknown languages and special knowledge will become useless. But love will last forever!

Let Us Pray

Father, I thank you for today and your son Jesus, who died on the cross over 2,000 years ago so we can experience the best love ever. Father, I pray for the wife, mother, sister, and/or daughter reading this. I pray you shall uproot all pain and past hurt in our life now. I decree and declare a healthy life for her right now in the name of Jesus. I pray for peace, Father, in the name of Jesus. I pray there will be no more nights she cries herself to sleep from pain but sow tears of joy because you, Father, have been faithful and merciful. Lord, I pray as you uproot every negative seed that you pour out love, joy, and peace. Father, remind her of who you called and created her to be. Father, remind her that she is beautiful daily as she grows to love herself again. Father, I thank you right now in the name of Jesus that all past hurt is dead, and as of today, she will not mourn it anymore but rejoice in being free to love and be loved in Jesus' majestic name. Amen.

What is your honest definition of love?

Do you have deep-rooted pain or hurt that has caused you not to operate in love? If so, how have you been dealing with it?

Do you want to be free from pain and hurt so you can experience the love you are missing?

Write down the things you are still holding on to and ask yourself whether those things are worth your life, peace, joy, and sanity? If they are not, drop them at the feet of Jesus.

_____

_____

_____

_____

_____

_____

_____

_____

_____

_____

_____

_____

Day 15
FAMILY

When I hear family, I just want to sing, "We are family … I got all my sisters and my brothers with me." My immediate family consists of my husband, children, parents, siblings, nieces, and nephews. Many times, we get married and believe that our spouse marries the entire family, or at least that's what is said in some families. In some marriages, that may work, while in others, it does not. Being able to separate your marriage from your family can be very hard at times. A meme circulating around social media asks, "If your husband and father get into an argument and your husband tells you to get in the car, but the father tells you differently, who would you listen to?"

Everybody has their own opinions about the question, as they should due to different views of the situation. I can answer honestly and say first I will try and help settle the situation, but I would have to listen to my husband. Because of our vows, we shared and understood our respectful roles in our marriage. We have to learn how to separate marriage and family. Some people's family can be so involved in their marriage that the marriage begins to crumble. That's why it is so important that you keep family out of your relationship. It is not true that once you marry, you marry the whole family because when times get rough and tough, God is the only one who can restore what once was. It's okay to tell your family to back up because when you decided to marry your spouse, you both became the new and improved family. As a wife, you cover your family just as well as your household. We have to pray earnestly for unity, peace, and joy among our families because the enemy thrives where there is division.

This is one of my favorite scriptures that keeps me grounded when it comes to my family:

Mark 10:7-8 (NIV)

'For this reason a man will leave his father and mother and be united to his wife, and the two will become one flesh.'

When was the last time you had to choose your spouse or family? I'm not saying you turn a blind eye if your spouse caused harm to your family. No, you do the right thing. The vows do state until death do you part. Are you in a place now where you're not sure what to do in tough situations regarding your family?

_____

_____

_____

_____

_____

_____

_____

_____

_____

_____

_____

_____

_____

_____

_____

Day 16

HOME

We have all heard home is where the heart is! A home is where you reside, where you are supposed to be at peace and safe. Keeping your house sacred is very important, like it is your own personal place and temple where you call all the shots. That's why it's very important to watch the traffic that comes in and out of your home. My husband cuts hair, and I constantly say his customers can't come through the house because spirits transfer and they do not care who they latch on to.

As a wife and mother, I like to create a spiritual atmosphere that no demon in hell can dwell in because I enjoy a peaceful house. So being able to pray and keep our home covered is very important to me. I'm reminded of Exodus 12:7, where they were told to take the sacrificial lamb' blood and place it on the doorpost. That was a sign so that when the death angel, sickness, etc. came, it would pass over those homes.

A friend told me that she and her husband have a declaration that they decree over their home, as well as a mission and vision statement. That blew my mind because I never thought to do that.

One of my favorite scriptures is Joshua 24:15:

And if it seem evil unto you to serve the LORD, choose you this day whom ye will serve; whether the gods which your fathers served that were beyond the River, or the gods of the Amorites, in whose land ye dwell: but as for me and my house, we will serve the LORD. (ESV)

Do you find time to go throughout your home to anoint every entryway? I challenge you to create a mission and vision statement over your home that can cause your home to shift in a way that would blow your mind and bring your home closer to God. Let that be a nightly declaration. God tells us we have not because we ask not. We must speak the things we declare and believe that they shall come to pass. Make sure to include the children in teaching the mission and vision statement for the house.

_____

_____

_____

_____

_____

_____

_____

_____

_____

_____

_____

_____

_____

_____

Day 17

LISTENING AND UNDERSTANDING

Listening and understanding a person can be hard, especially when it comes to being married. We sometimes listen without understanding, and I'm a firm believer that in order to understand, we must first have knowledge of the person or situation. As a wife, I can be listening and not understand due to not having clarity of the point being made. My husband will say, "Just listen," but the thing is, I'm listening. Can I say I'm not understanding?

Two quick examples: You can tell me (I'm listening) the ingredients for baking a homemade Bundt cake, but if you never explain why I cannot over stir or use fewer ingredients than needed, the cake will not come out as it should due to a lack of understanding. I'm sure a person will look at the cake and say, "You were not listening," but in reality, I was listening. I did not understand because the steps weren't precise.

The second example is my son; it takes a whole lot of knowledge to understand everything he does. The school called me and said that he was in the office due to a situation in class. As the principal talked, I listened. To me, it made no sense because he was unsure himself. So I said to the principal, "I'm not understanding," and asked if he could explain. He began to explain that my son got upset due to the teacher not listening to him. While getting upset with the teacher which was not acceptable, I totally understood that, so we began to talk and listen to my son explain the situation and give clarity. He stated one of his classmates had come to him because she was being picked on. He went to the teacher because he knew the girl talked about killing herself. The teacher responded that it was okay, and to keep his nose out of their business. That made him upset because he knew the things the classmate had been through. The principal said to me, "Mom, I totally understand it." He said we cannot be so quick to listen without having the knowledge needed to understand the whole situation.

That's why it is important to pray for our children daily. The attacks are real, and the enemy tries every plot, ploy, and twist to deter your thoughts daily. We must pray for understanding not just for ourselves, but our husbands, children, and those we may come in contact with on a daily basis. We should pray that God shall incline our ears to hear, listen (take in), and understand (digest).

Proverbs 2:3-5 (NKJV)

Yes, if you cry out for discernment,
And lift up your voice for understanding,

If you seek her as silver,
And search for her as *for* hidden treasures;

Then you will understand the fear of the LORD,
And find the knowledge of God.

Have you ever not understood something and the person got upset? If so, how did it make you feel?

Were you able to explain to the person that you were listening, but they didn't give enough information, which caused you not to understand them?

How important is listening and understanding in your marriage or relationship?

_____

_____

_____

_____

_____

_____

_____

_____

_____

_____

_____

_____

_____

Day 18
COMMUNICATION

Communication is key in our everyday life. Poor communication in relationships can be a disaster waiting to happen. For many years, I pushed and pushed my husband to talk about problems with his family, job, or our household. He would say he was okay or there was no problem, which made me furious. Some people aren't good at communicating, and others may speak everything on their minds. I'm others (lol). I just learned through trial that poor communication can lead to depression, especially if the communication is not good in relationships. Communication is the exchange of information, sending and receiving.

People think the only way they can express things is verbally, but we have text messages, email, and can even take it back to pen and paper. As a child, if I needed to get something off my heart, I would write my mom a letter because I feared what she would say in response. At that time in my life, that worked for me. I believe my husband would rather text because he can get a lot out without me cutting him off (which shows poor communication). Everybody should be able to communicate without being interrupted. I pray all the time that God will help me communicate in a way that is understandable to the person receiving it.

Proverbs 13:17 (NLT)
An unreliable messenger stumbles into trouble, but a reliable messenger brings healing.

Proverbs 18:21 (NLT)

The tongue can bring death or life; those who love to talk will reap the consequences.

Colossians 4:6 (NLT)

Let your conversation be gracious and attractive so that you will have the right response for everyone.

How is communication within your marriage or relationship?

Would you like to improve communication within your marriage? If so, I suggest that you seek God and ask him to help you to learn your spouse's way of communicating.

_____

_____

_____

_____

_____

_____

_____

_____

_____

_____

_____

_____

_____

_____

_____

_____

Day 19

TRUST

The word trust gets thrown around so much that it has caused so many problems in marriages. Lack of trust leads to divorces and affairs and can also lead to health problems caused by stress or depression. People say it is hard to trust in areas that have caused pain or even trust people who have been disloyal. I do agree, but we must be able to forgive so we will not be bound to the deceit of people. Deception is one of the enemy's biggest tactics. It's his business to cause us as people to lack trust—just as he got Eve to break her trust in Adam and God by going against the Word of God.

We have heard the saying "trust no man?" But then we are told to trust our spouses. That is hard to do when spouses and people are not worthy of trust. We just want to do what is right. I remember when God shared with me, "It is not your husband or people who you are trusting." He stated that flesh will fail you every time, but it is the spirit of God; it is me in him or them; it is the Holy Spirit who we shall trust in man. At that point, it made all things clearer because if I trust God, I trust that everything will be fine. In trusting the spirit of God in my husband or people, they must do right, and anything that needs to be revealed, God will reveal. The Bible tells us that God is not a liar (Numbers 23:19) and that his word shall not return void (Isaiah 55:11).

So learning to trust your spouse again after a bad situation could be hard and trying, but know God did not give up on you. Remember when you trust God, he will protect you from all harm and hurt. It's okay to trust your spouse again. God is forever faithful to those who trust him in the midst of. Nothing goes unseen or heard in trusting God.

Proverbs 3:5 (AMP)

Trust in and rely confidently on the Lord with all your heart; and do not rely on your own insight or understanding.

Do you lack trust in God? Do you lack trust in your spouse? If so, are you willing to trust again? I know it can be hard after being hurt, but I suggest forgiving your spouse so you can trust God in your spouse.

_____

_____

_____

_____

_____

_____

_____

_____

_____

_____

_____

_____

_____

_____

_____

_____

Day 20
MARRIAGE

What is marriage? It is the forming of a sacred union recognized between two people, a lifelong covenant relationship under God.

We all have heard "marriage is not for the weak," and it's most definitely not. I believe the first to fifth years are the hardest. I believe you find out more about the person when you say "I do," or is it a test of your vows to one another? My husband and I have been married for ten years as of November 5, 2021. For the first five years, it seemed unreal to me that I was married. It wasn't until 2015 that what I believed to be a dream became a reality. I do not take my marriage for granted at all, even during the trying times. I have most definitely learned to seek God and not people. I have learned to pray on a level like never before concerning my marriage.

As women, we always want to make sure that the marriage is our first and last marriage. You know, like our dream king has arrived. Sometimes that is not the case, especially if you have not sought God on your soon-to-be spouse's behalf. I remember walking down the aisle praying to the Lord to send me to my husband because I did not want to be married to someone else's husband. One Sunday in church during prayer, our pastor was ministering and said, "Treva, stop asking God to send you your husband because he already has." I could have hit the floor or slid down the wall because that was something I was praying secretly. I have seen the damage of being married to the wrong person and what it could do. I just did not want that for myself.

Seek God before you say I do; ask God to show you more than the material things. Once you become married, it is no longer "I" but "we." You become a member of a lifelong team that will need practices and camps to continue to function as such. You will learn to cover each other during the most detrimental times, whether you want to or not. We all have heard that when you marry the husband or wife, you marry the whole family (inserts scream). I really dislike that saying because when bills are due, the family is not there. When either of you needs each other, the family is not there. The Bible tells us that the husband leaves his mother and father (family) to cleave to his wife, and vice versa. You are now one with your spouse, and neither of you is married to the family (let's just be clear). Now we might have to deal with some things each family does, but never let family tear apart what's sacred to God. Never allow family to make you choose between them and your spouse.

Mark 10:9 (NKJV)

Therefore what God has joined, let no man separate.

Are you seeking to be married, or have you accepted the ring and now you are trying to figure out some things? Have you sought God for this big change in your life? Are you and your spouse having family problems, wherein they seem to insert themselves in your marriage? If so, have you talked with your spouse? If you have not, are you willing to have the conversation? Praying that God opens my spouse's eyes to the problem has always worked for me. God is willing to meet every marriage need.

_____

_____

_____

_____

_____

_____

_____

_____

_____

_____

_____

_____

_____

Day 21

TEMPTATION

Many people in marriages do not want to discuss temptation. It is swept under the rug because no one wants to be real about it. Everyone has been tempted on some level. Maybe it was temptation while on a diet, cheating on a test, stealing, or **cheating on your spouse** (whhaaaaaaat). All of those temptations are real and can ruin you in some way. I remember asking my husband if he had ever been tempted (lol). This was when we first got married like a year in. His reply was no, but I didn't buy it because we are all tempted. Jesus was tempted. So if Jesus can be tempted, it leaves room for those of us on earth.

Wikipedia defines temptation as *a desire to engage in short-term urges for enjoyment that threatens long-term goals.*

The dictionary defines temptation as *the desire to do something, especially something wrong or unwise or a thing or course of action that attracts or tempts someone.*

So after reading those definitions, those who stated they have never been tempted must admit to those temptations. We can lie to man all day, but the Father who sits in heaven sees and knows all. Sad to say, many marriages are torn apart due to temptation, which is introduced by lust. Temptation and lust are twins; you can't have one without the other, and they can be tricky. Sometimes they act as fraternal while other times identical. Your marriage and relationship with God are sacred. Do not allow the enemy to come in and destroy what God has joined together. The Bible tells us that what God joined, nothing can come against. Temptation and lust are the weapons that formed, but God said they shall not prosper.

Matthew 6:13 (NIV)

And lead us not into temptation, but deliver us from the evil one.

Luke 22:40 (NIV)

…Pray that you will not fall into temptation.

1 Corinthians 10:13 (ESV)

No temptation has overtaken you that is not common to man. God is faithful, and he will not let you be tempted beyond your ability, but with the temptation he will also provide the way of escape, that you may be able to endure it.

Have you been in a place of temptation? If so, how did you handle it?
Did you acknowledge your exit? Have you forgiven yourself?

_____

_____

_____

_____

_____

_____

_____

_____

_____

_____

_____

_____

_____

_____

_____

_____

To My Sisters in Christ:

Now that you have finished this twenty-one day devotional, I pray that God will continue to cover and protect you. I pray that you have been able to heal from past situations and have grown in ways you did not think were possible. I pray something you read during these past twenty-one days caused a shift in not just your life but, your home and those you came in contact with. I pray joy, love, peace, romance, restoration, and forgiveness were released on your behalf. I pray because of your vulnerability and transparency, God was able to renew, refresh, and revive you. May you continue your prayer journey, yet this is just the beginning in Jesus' name.

Again, I thank you for your purchase and for allowing me to share what God has placed on my heart with you.

~ *Treva J.*

Ways to connect:

Instagram: therestorationcoach

Facebook: Restoring, Empowering, & Caring Life Coaching

Website: www.trevaj.com

About the Author

Treva J is a native of Pineville, Louisiana and the wife of the awesome Staff Sergeant Vernon James and mother of three beautiful children. She has a passion to motivate, uplift, and inspire those she comes in contact with, but her purpose is to serve people. Treva is a certified Christian life coach, speaker, God-called intercessor, prayer warrior, and victim advocate. She has been granted the opportunity to meet and share her testimony with new people due to travel with the US Army. Treva has a global voice that has inspired many people thus far. Her superpowers are worshiping God, prayer, and evangelizing the Word of God. Treva believes if she can reach one life, she has made a difference.

Connect and Share

If you enjoyed this book, please purchase copies for other women in your life, and leave a review online at amazon.com, barnesandnoble. com, and goodreads.com.

Connect with Author Treva J at www.trevaj.com or on social media:

Instagram: therestorationcoach

Facebook: Restoring, Empowering, & Caring Life Coaching